LEADERSHIP
IN THREE MORE WORDS

The Art and Science of
Educational Leadership
with Heart in Mind

Michelle McQueen-Williams, Ph.D.

Leadership in Three More Words: The Art and Science of Educational Leadership with Heart in Mind

Copyright © 2025 by Michelle McQueen-Williams

Printed in the United States of America

All rights reserved. No part of this publication may be used or reproduced, stored in a retrieval system or transmitted in any way by any means, electronic, mechanical, photocopy, recording or otherwise without the prior permission of the author except as provided by USA copyright law.

For permissions or bulk orders please address correspondence to: mcqueen722@gmail.com

ISBN: 978-1-7363189-1-1

DEDICATED TO...

My son, Mr. Byron Williams who taught me what unconditional love means.

TABLE OF CONTENTS

Introduction: The Heart of the Work 1

1. Heart to Heart 11

2. Hard to Reach? 23

3. What's the Matter? 33

4. Yes, They Can! 41

5. They Don't Drive! 49

6. The Parent Appeal 55

7. It's About Them 63

8. The Leadership Challenge: 71

About the Author 79

Endnotes 81

INTRODUCTION: THE HEART OF THE WORK

It's been five years since I published my first book, *Leadership in Three Words*, and in that time, so much has changed—in the world, in education, and in me. Since that book's release, I've received phenomenal feedback! I've had countless conversations with educators, administrators, and students, all of which have deepened my understanding of what it means to lead in today's educational climate. And if there's one truth that's held steady through it all, it's this: relationships still matter—perhaps more than anything else.

Since 2020, after transitioning out of a formal leadership role in K–12 education, I've been working with undergraduate students at Virginia Union University who aspire to become a part of the teaching profession. Although my day-to-day work looks different, I'm still deeply connected to K–12 through consulting, mentoring, and advocacy. What I've come to see, more clearly than ever, is that whether we're working with children, teens, or young adults, *connection is the common thread*. It's the make-or-break factor in whether students engage, whether they learn, and ultimately, whether they thrive.

When I think about the challenges educators face today, especially when trying to reach students who've been labeled "difficult" or "disengaged, I'm reminded that at the core, the need is the same: to be seen, heard, and valued. What I'm doing now with undergraduates – helping them build confidence, see their potential, and believe in their future—isn't all that different from what I did in a high school classroom. It's still heart work.

This became even more evident to me during the Covid-19 pandemic. I joined Virginia Union in 2020, right in the thick of it. Classes were online, students were disconnected, and engagement was at an all-time low. What stood out immediately was how essential connection still was—virtual or not. The students who were just logging in without truly being present were missing something vital. However, once I had the chance to connect one-on-one when we talked beyond the screen and built real relationships. That's when they started to care. That's when they showed up, not just physically but emotionally and mentally.

> ### Science Snippet...
> According to the National Center for Education Statistics, during the COVID-19 pandemic, many students experienced significant academic setbacks due to remote learning. National data revealed sharp declines in math and reading scores, especially among elementary and middle school students. However, when students returned to in-person learning, outcomes began to improve, with the greatest gains seen in schools that prioritized consistent instruction, engagement, and strong teacher-student relationships.[1]

Even now, years later, K–12 students are still recovering. They're rebuilding social skills and relearning how to connect with peers and teachers. That means we, as educators and leaders, have to work even harder—not just to deliver content, but to *reach hearts*. Without connection, curriculum won't stick. Without relationships, students won't rise.

I've seen this truth play out again and again. Recently, I was honored with the Mary McLeod Bethune Trailblazer Award, and one of my former students from the early 2000s showed up at the banquet. He had once been labeled a "challenging" student, but I always preferred "student of promise" because language matters. He went on to graduate from a technical program with a 3.0 GPA and is now both an electrician and a real estate broker, the same broker who sold me my current home. Nearly thirty years later, we're still connected. Why? Because of relationships.

That moment brought something into sharp focus: when former students see me, they don't talk about the lessons I taught—they talk about how I made them feel. That's the part they remember. The same thing happened when I ran into another former student while getting a B12 shot at the pharmacy. As I stepped up to the counter, the young woman behind it looked at me wide-eyed and said, "Ms. McQueen, do you remember me? You were my teacher in high school!"

At first, I didn't recognize her. But then she told me her first name, and instantly, her last name came right back to me. I blurted it out before she could even say it. "Yes!" she said, beaming. "That's me!"

What she remembered wasn't a subject-verb agreement lesson or a writing strategy. What came back to her was the quote I used to say all the time from Vernon Brundage Jr.: *"Excuses are the tools of incompetence used to build bridges to nowhere and monuments of nothingness, and those who use them seldom specialize in anything else."* She said, "You used to tell us that all the time!"

She also remembered my high heels clicking down the hallway and our Monday morning "fireside chats," which were moments before I actually began teaching when I'd let students share whatever was on their minds. It was our chance to connect, to talk about the weekend, and to clear whatever was weighing them down before diving into academics. I called it "reaching before teaching." They could talk about whatever was bothering them, and I would listen. They call it "morning meetings" now.

That day at the pharmacy, the two of us stood there just talking and reminiscing, even though I had an appointment waiting. She didn't recall a single academic lesson I had taught, but she remembered how she felt in my class. She remembered being seen, heard, and uplifted. That's the legacy of heart work.

It's also what inspired me to write this book. I wanted to return to the conversation I started in my first book and go deeper. That first book was received incredibly well. It's still selling and continues to shift the way people approach leadership in schools. I've had readers tell me it changed the way they lead. One principal shared that he lives by the concept of "trust and verify." Others were moved by chapters like *Heart Work* and *Lead and Lift*, which emphasized the importance of investing in both students and staff—not just through policy and procedure, but through presence, empathy, and connection.

One colleague told me that *Lead and Lift* opened her eyes to something simple but profound: we often ask educators to do everything they *have* to do, but we forget to support them in doing what they *want* to do. That sense of being valued, of being seen as more than just a worker, is what makes people stay. That's what makes them thrive. That's what leadership with heart in mind looks like.

Yet, too often in education, we focus almost entirely on the science of teaching—lesson planning, pedagogy, and classroom management. All of that is necessary. But what's missing is the *art*. The heart. And when we ignore that side of the work, we risk creating environments where students go unnoticed, where teachers burn out, and where learning feels transactional instead of transformational.

Since publishing my first book, the world has gone through a global pandemic, rising political tensions, and a concern about the decline in funding for critical educational programs. Title I schools could lose support. Pre-K programs are being cut—even though research clearly shows that children who attend pre-K are far more likely to go to college. Meal programs that meet students' basic needs are slated to be reduced. These aren't just policies; they are life-altering decisions that affect whether a child is ready to learn or even wants to come to school.

There are some real-world consequences I foresee because of pending education funding cuts—consequences that impact not just schools, but entire communities. When budgets are reduced, it's often student services that suffer first. The loss of critical staff, such as school counselors, has a direct effect on students, especially those who are already underserved or have experienced trauma. These professionals provide vital social and emotional support that can't be replaced by a textbook or worksheet. Without them, students may fall through the cracks, dropout rates could increase, and the educational environment becomes less responsive to the whole child.

These potential outcomes concern me deeply. Without intervention, the students who need the most will be left with the least. If we don't approach this work with heart, if we don't recognize that connection is as vital as content, we will continue to fail the very students we claim to serve.

This work is deeply personal for me. As a woman of faith, I see this work as a calling--as ministry. Leadership is more than a role; it's a form of service. For me, it's rooted in the belief that we are here to love, to lift, and to lead others well. As a child, I had access to programs and people who believed in me before I could believe in myself. They saw my potential and poured into me. With love, they went the extra mile and lifted me. And because of them, I was able to build a life I never imagined. That's what I strive to do for others. I see the spark in students, and I want to be the one who fans it into flame.

Because connection isn't just a feel-good concept, it's preparation. It shapes a student's sense of self and what they believe they can become. As Rita Pierson once said, *"Every child deserves a champion—an adult who will never give up on them, who understands the power of connection."* I always show her "Every Kid Needs a Champion" video when I teach or train educators. One of the most powerful moments is when she shares how a student who got 18 wrong and 2 right was praised for the "+2" instead of scolded for the "-18." That shift in perspective, that focus on possibilities—that's what heart work is all about.

Pierson's words offer more than just inspiration; they outline a path we as educators can choose daily. Turning her philosophy into practice is not complicated, but it does require intentionality. It means reevaluating how we approach everything from grading to relationships. Do we see students' progress as a win, even if they're not yet on grade level? Are we celebrating the child who moves from a Level 1 to a Level 2 in reading? That's growth and it matters.

It also means offering grace in the moments when students struggle. For example, when I was a classroom teacher, I implemented "Make-Up Fridays," giving students the opportunity to complete missed assignments instead of leaving them with zeros they couldn't recover from. A simple shift from an all-or-nothing mindset to one focused on opportunity and redemption can be transformational. As educators, we can choose to connect first and correct later. Grace and compassion shouldn't be afterthoughts; they should be priorities, just as we would hope for when life gets tough for us.

It may sound cliché, but our children are the future. Whether they're in kindergarten or college, they will inherit the systems, communities, and world we leave behind. And with more of my years behind me than ahead, I can't help but ask,

Who are we preparing them to be? What kind of world are we shaping for them—and with them? That's what this book is about at its core.

This book is a call for educators and leaders in education to remember what matters most. It's a call to return to the heart. In addition to being an educator and leader, I'm also an ordained minister, and my orientation is deeply rooted in the Christian faith. So, while this book is designed to teach you how to return to the heart based on insights and lessons gained through years of professional experience, I hope it does more than feed your mind; I hope it feeds your spirit. You'll find traces of faith woven throughout these pages, because that's who I am. At the same time, I've included research and data that affirm what many of us in education already know in our hearts: this work is deep and meaningful, and science backs it up. It is the intersection of the skills and science of teaching with the art and heart of the work that equips us to do the job well. It's the connection, the relationships, the care that make the work worth doing. And this work is, indeed, worthwhile. Now, let's learn how to do the work, leading with the heart in mind.

HEART TO HEART

Heart to Heart is more than a three-word phrase; it's a mindset, a way of leading, teaching, and connecting. It speaks not just to educators, but to anyone who has influence in a young person's life: teachers, school leaders, professors, and mentors. To teach effectively, we must lead from the heart. We must meet students where they are—not just academically, but emotionally, socially, and even spiritually. This is *heart work*, not just hard work.

Too often, we expect students to perform simply because we asked. Some will. Some will do their homework, show up on time, and raise their hands and follow instructions. But what about the others? What about the student who didn't bring their homework? Is the goal to punish them or to teach them?

I once stood in the back of a classroom and watched a student sit silently at his desk, empty-handed, while others were engaged with reviewing their homework. He hadn't done the assignment, and the teacher refused to give him a worksheet to follow along. Her logic? He didn't do the work, so he doesn't get to participate. My heart said otherwise. My heart asked, *What is he going to learn staring at a blank desk? If he's disconnected now, how long before he checks out completely?* I asked the teacher, "Can he at least look on with a classmate?" She was hesitant. But this wasn't about policy. It was about perspective. It was about *empathy*, or the lack thereof. It was about seeing the child, not just the behavior.

Heart to heart means that I see your need, and I don't make you feel less than because you have one. It means I check in with you. I ask, "Are you okay?" I offer, "Do you want to sit next to someone and look on?" I seek connection, not just compliance.

In higher education, I see the same principle play out. My college students are expected to observe classrooms for course credit. When a student tells me they're having trouble with transportation, my head says, *Tell them to figure it out*. My heart says, *Let's figure it out together*. Maybe they need bus fare. Maybe they need an Uber. Life is still "life-ing," even in college.

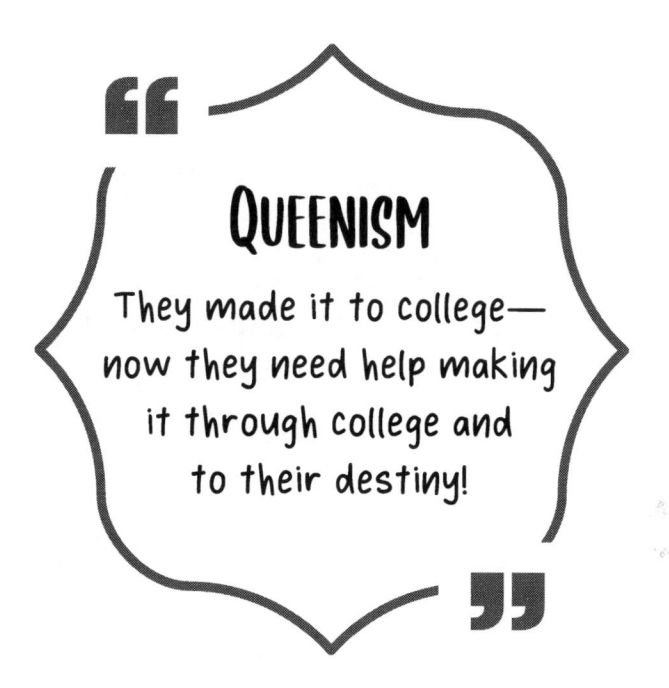

> # QUEENISM
> They made it to college—now they need help making it through college and to their destiny!

Empathy in Action

Delivering education without empathy is not just ineffective, it's unethical. Empathy is not sympathy. It's not "I feel sorry for you." It's "I see you. I hear you. I care." It's understanding how a student might feel and being willing to adjust your approach accordingly.

> ### Science Snippet...
> Empathy isn't just a soft skill; it's a powerful teaching tool. Research shows that when teachers consistently show empathy, students are more likely to be engaged, motivated, and resilient in the face of academic challenges. Empathy helps build trust, reduces anxiety, and creates a classroom environment where students feel safe to learn and grow.[2]

There's a well-known saying (often attributed to Theodore Roosevelt) that says, *"People don't care how much you know until they know how much you care."* We must lead with care before we can lead with instructional content. We must get to know them for who they are before they give us permission to shape who they will become. I believe that every child is fearfully and wonderfully made, and as leaders, we are stewards of their potential. Seeing them clearly is not just good practice; it's a matter of our purpose as leaders in education.

Teacher preparation programs often focus on cultural competence, but this is different from empathy. Empathy and cultural competency are not the same, though both are essential in effective leadership and education. Cultural competency equips us to recognize, understand, and respect the differences between cultures. Empathy, on the other hand, allows us to emotionally connect with others by becoming aware of the experiences they are living culturally, emotionally, and socially. While cultural competency helps us see the *what*, empathy helps us feel the *why*.

Thus, empathy goes deeper than cultural competence. It's not just about understanding backgrounds; it's about learning our students, bonding, listening, and showing up for them with humanity. Some educators say, *"I'm just here to do my job."* However, teaching is not just a job. It's a calling. It's a "feeling" business. If you can't feel, you can't teach effectively.

Empathy can be learned. This is why I believe teacher training programs should intentionally embed empathy into their curriculum. This can be done by incorporating experiences, real-world scenarios, and case studies that give aspiring educators the chance to actively practice empathy. Adding these elements wouldn't require an overhaul, just thoughtful integration into existing courses such as ethics or culturally responsive teaching. These moments of practice can help future educators better understand and connect with the diverse students they will serve.

Even if operating with empathy doesn't come naturally, I encourage you to make an intentional effort. Step into your students' world. Go to their neighborhoods. Talk to their families. Visit their homes, if you're allowed. Understand their lives beyond the walls of your classroom. That's the real work. *That's* heart work.

A Learning Moment: "You're So Smart, You're Stupid"

I once had a ninth-grade student who got in trouble for throwing something in class. I was a new administrator, and I came in ready to "handle it." I said, "You almost hit that girl with that protractor!"

He replied, "You're so smart, you're stupid. That wasn't a protractor—it was a compass rose."

That stopped me in my tracks. In that moment, I realized I had come in all head, no heart. I hadn't even asked him what happened. I assumed. I judged. And I was wrong.

That student checked me. And in doing so, he taught me. If I had paused to ask questions, if I had led with heart, the conversation would have gone very differently. He was being teased. What I saw was a reaction, not the cause. I never questioned the other student, only him.

Every student—every person—deserves due process. Everyone deserves to be heard. Especially those who are often misunderstood or mislabeled. Heart to heart means listening, even when you think you already know the answer.

Say Their Names

Connection starts with something as simple as a name. In light of this, I encourage any teacher or education leader to learn the names of your students. Say them often. Use them with care. It matters. There's a difference between yelling,

"Stop running!" and gently calling out, "Stop running, **Peyton**!" Names make things personal. Names say, "I see you. You belong."

> ### Science Snippet...
> Studies show that in school settings, when educators consistently use students' names, it fosters a stronger sense of belonging, respect, and personal connection. Students are more likely to engage in learning and demonstrate positive behavior when they feel seen and known. Neuroscience even shows that hearing one's name activates unique areas of the brain tied to identity and emotional response; it lights something up inside. A name isn't just a label; it's a doorway to relationship.[3]

I once had a student with a French name: "Javier." I couldn't pronounce well, so I gave her a nickname: "J Love." Her face would light up every time I said it! It was our bond. I made it a point, as a principal, to learn the name of every student. I'd sit with kindergarten kids at lunch just to practice. People would say, "She knows everybody's name." That wasn't by accident. I worked on it.

And it wasn't just students. I learned teachers' names, their kids' names, and their birthdays. When you say someone's name, you tell them, *You matter*.

> **QUEENISM**
>
> Little people that matter grow up to be big people that care about what matters most.

Wraparound Love

Teaching is more than what happens between the bells. It's about the *wraparound*—the whole child, the whole family, the whole community. What do your students love? Basketball? Science? Video games? Love it with them.

I'd say to a student, "You're sleepy today—been gaming all night?" They'd laugh, but it opened a door. I'd show up at their basketball games on Saturdays. On Monday, they'd say, "Ms. McQueen came to the game!" That mattered a great deal to them. I'd bring my own son to the game, talk to the coach, talk to the parents, and be a part of the community, connecting with the people.

> ### Science Snippet...
> Research from the American Psychological Association indicates that when students have positive relationships with their teachers, they exhibit better academic performance and social development. These relationships foster a sense of belonging and motivation, which are crucial for student success.[4]

If something went wrong, I had the relationship to say, "Should I call Coach James?" That wasn't a threat – it was community. It was accountability wrapped in love. I knew their pastors, their churches, and their mentors. If they were getting baptized, I showed up. *That's* heart to heart.

Ultimately, the lesson I desire to leave with you is to let the heart lead the head. Let empathy guide your decisions. Let names, stories, and connections be your curriculum. This is Heart Work. This is how we change the lives of students—heart to heart.

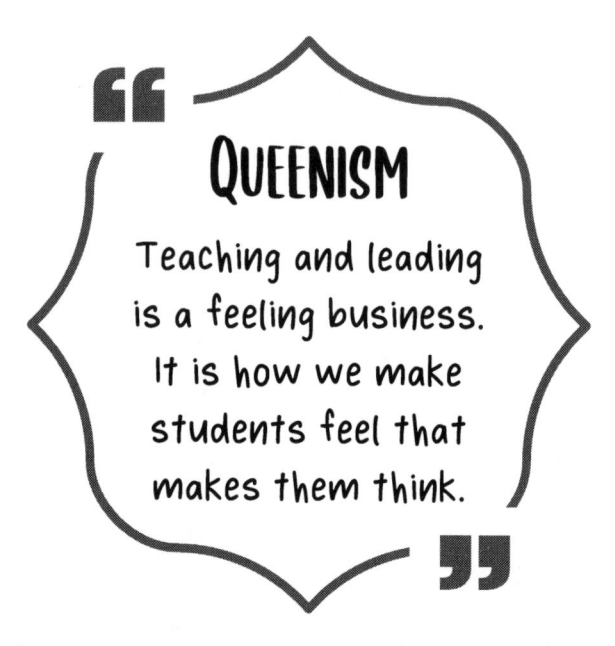

> **QUEENISM**
>
> Teaching and leading is a feeling business. It is how we make students feel that makes them think.

When Schedules Compete with Connection

Just so you know, I am fully aware that systemic barriers like high-stakes testing and rigid school schedules often stand in the way of heart-centered teaching and leading. I've been an educator for over three decades, so I know the reality of balancing the rigors of instruction with connection. Teachers and administrators can become so consumed with testing protocols and accreditation demands that it drains the joy right out of the work. Yes, we need to know what students are learning, but we can do that while also doing the heart work that helps them love learning.

Scheduling is another challenge. There's simply not enough time in the day. Intentional programming like morning meetings or fireside chats can build connection and community among teachers, students, and administrators.

But when something has to be cut to keep up with the pace of the curriculum, this is often the first thing to go. And that's a loss we can't afford.

Doing whatever it takes to connect with students, even when it's hard, is the mark of an impactful educator, no matter your role. Yes, educators and school leaders are busy. There are schedules to manage, curriculum to cover, data to track. But connection must remain a priority. I've seen it done time and time again by those who are simply determined to do it. The ones who understand how significant connection is find a way. As for those who aren't willing to go the extra mile, well, you'll hear it in their words: "They don't pay me enough to do both... I'm either going to teach and help them hit the metrics, or I'll try to connect with them, but I'm not wearing myself out trying to do both." But the truth is, the kids deserve both.

Remember: this isn't just a job; it's a calling. Part of that call is leading with empathy. Empathy shapes the way students see themselves, see each other, and see the world around them. I've watched students grow up and go on to serve in fields like mental health counseling, open group homes, and become case workers for youth in crisis. That kind of career path doesn't come out of nowhere. It begins with someone showing them empathy and modeling what it means to care.

HARD TO REACH?

"Hard to reach" is a label we often give students who challenge our systems, who don't fit neatly into our routines or expectations. But the truth is, when we say a child is hard to reach, we need to pause and ask ourselves—*why?*

I first met a young man in the early 2000s who was labeled exactly that: hard to reach. Bright. Bold. Brilliant. He challenged teachers, not out of defiance, but because he *knew* things. One day, he corrected a teacher who had given the wrong answer to the class. Instead of honoring his knowledge, she sent him to the office. He didn't react well, and that moment shaped how other teachers and administrators in the school saw him. Yet, I saw something different. This was a student who wasn't being intellectually challenged. He didn't need punishment; he needed purpose. Years later, that same young man became a successful real estate broker. In fact, he sold me the house that I live in today. People once said he was hard to reach, but I know now that he wasn't unreachable; he was underserved. His capabilities were mismanaged.

When students struggle or disengage, our job is not to write them off. It's to ask, *What's the story behind the struggle?* Are they facing challenges at home? Are they bored? Hurt? Hungry? Traumatized? Overlooked? Are they simply in need of someone to see them—*really* see them?

Take virtual learning, for example. We ask students to turn on their cameras and just show up. But what if they've been evicted? What if they don't have Wi-Fi or a quiet place to sit, read, and study? It's not always about defiance. Sometimes, it's about survival. And in those moments, we've got to choose compassion over compliance. Sometimes, that looks like giving them extra time. Sometimes, it means dropping off materials. Sometimes, it just means saying, *"Come see me when things settle down."*

Inspiring Intrinsic Motivation

Rather than being so quick to label students as "uninspired," "difficult" or "hard to reach," let's give them the benefit of the doubt and take time to dig beneath the surface to investigate what's really going on with them. When you discover the real story of what's happening or the root of why they are behaving or performing the way they do, you can use this knowledge as a starting point for how to intervene and inspire them. However, you'll never be able to inspire them or motivate them until you care enough to resist labeling them and get involved in knowing and connecting with them.

The starting point for every educator and leader in education, when they experience a student most people would be inclined to label, should be, *This student is capable of being inspired and producing desirable learning outcomes.* There are real, practical ways educators can spark intrinsic motivation in students, especially those who feel disconnected. It begins with something simple but powerful: believing in them and making sure they know it.

When a student knows you see potential in them, it changes everything. That belief can be shown in small but consistent ways like spending one-on-one time before a quiz or test, checking in during the day, or setting up systems like a morning "check-in/check-out" where students have a go-to adult before they face the day. These aren't grand gestures; they're intentional acts that remind students they're seen, valued, and supported. When students feel this, they begin to believe in themselves.

Going the extra mile is a choice. It's about inserting yourself into the space of a child to intervene and ensure they have what they need to succeed. It's about making yourself visible and present to them as a resource to them so they know they don't have to struggle or journey alone. For many students, this is the difference-maker that will determine the success or failure of their academic pursuits. It will determine whether they remain in school, flunk out, or walk out, determining that school just isn't for them. As leaders in education, we can't just say, "That's their choice!" Instead, we must care and make ourselves available to them. I'm reminded of Jesus' example. He didn't wait for people to come to Him. He went to them. Our presence in the lives of children must be intentional, just like His was for us.

I sleep well at night knowing I've done all I can to help a student succeed. I can't make them walk the path—but I can light the way. And often, when they feel seen and supported, they will take that step. I've seen what happens when students are truly seen; there is a transformation that takes place like you wouldn't believe, especially among the students that people have written off or all but thrown away. This reminds me of the biblical principle of grace (I told you I was an ordained minister), offering kindness even when it's not deserved. Some students need grace before they ever give us growth.

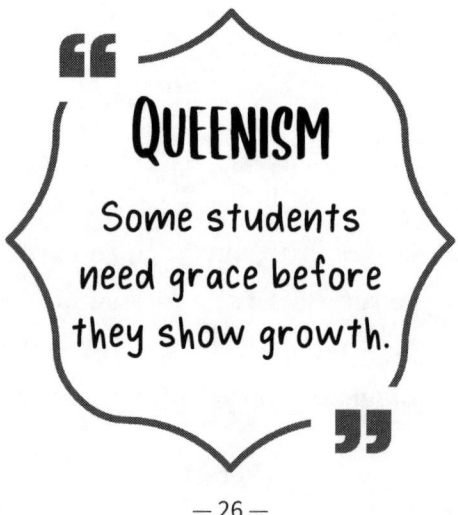

> **QUEENISM**
> Some students need grace before they show growth.

I once mentored a girl with disruptive behavior. She was smart and strong-willed, and the school labeled her difficult. But I made a deal: "If you make it through the week without disrupting class, I'll paint your nails on Friday." She showed up every day, held it together, and on Friday, we painted nails. She waited all day for that moment because she believed that I was going to do what I told her I would do. Because I kept my word, we built trust. Years later, she graduated high school with her own business. She was never hard to reach. She just needed someone to reach her *differently*.

> ### Science Snippet...
> According to the American Psychological Association, students who feel connected to their teachers are more likely to engage in learning and exhibit positive behaviors. This connection can be especially beneficial for students facing emotional or behavioral challenges.[5]

When teachers or leaders tell me a student is hard to reach, I ask, "Tell me more about that." Sometimes, we're trying to reach students the way *we* prefer, not the way *they* need. The Golden Rule says to treat people how you want to be treated. I take this a step further and say that we should treat people how *they* want to be treated. The damage we do with that "hard to reach" label is immeasurable. Students start to believe it. They disengage. They drop out. Their spark dims. And yet, I've watched the same student cause chaos in one class and shine in another. Why? Because one teacher or leader connected, and the other didn't. Connection changes behavior. Never forget this!

As a mother of a son with autism, I've had to fight hard all his life to ensure he was treated fairly. He's done it all—sports, choir, gainful employment—but many only saw his disabilities, not his unique *abilities*. I've watched teachers punish him instead of empowering him. I remember once when my son had forgotten his band shoes on a *Wednesday*. That *Saturday*, which was senior night at the school football game, he was benched while the rest of the band members went out on a break to go get a snack from the concession stand. I saw my son sitting over on the bleachers all alone and went to ask him what was going on, and when he explained that the band director told him he couldn't go get a snack with his bandmates because he'd forgotten his shoes days ago, I was livid. I knew the impact of what was happening to him then and how long-lasting the impact would be in his life. He, on the other hand, didn't even realize the harm being done to him with such a penalty, which didn't fit the offense. In fact, he had no hard feelings; he still liked the teacher. I told him to get up and go join his bandmates at the concession stand. As both a mother and an educator, that moment taught me how easily those small slights can take place. Sometimes, educators carry their own past hurts into the classroom and take them out on students. That's not education. That's projection.

One of the greatest challenges in education is making sure we truly see students for who they are, not just through the lens of our own experiences or past. That requires self-awareness, reflection, and a willingness to set aside personal baggage. As a school leader, I often told my staff, "Whatever happened before you walked into this building, leave it at the door." If you had an argument at home, leave it in the parking lot. If a student interaction triggers something from your own upbringing, consider leaning on resources like employee assistance programs. The truth is, we all carry things. But if we're not intentional, we can unintentionally project that onto the very students we're trying to serve. We owe it to our kids to show up fully present. They deserve the best version of us every day. And that means being mindful, reflective, and ready to serve with fresh eyes and an open heart.

As an educator or a leader in education, I'm sure you've said that you got into this work to make a difference. You certainly didn't do it for the money or the prestige. You did it to make an impact. You don't make an impact by grading papers. You do it by building bridges. So, the next time you're tempted to say a student is hard to reach, I encourage you to *reflect*. Are they hard to reach, or are we trying to reach them the wrong way?

Who's Crying Now?

I once taught a fourth-grade student who cried every single day. He was taller than the others and stood out. The kids picked on him relentlessly. People said he was hard to reach, but I saw a child in pain. So, I spent time with him—in the cafeteria, on the playground, and talking to his parents. I made an effort to connect with him. I told him, "When you cry, those kids work even harder to make you cry. But they're only doing it because they're jealous of how smart and tall you are!" Slowly, things changed. He gained confidence. He became a star high school football player. Today, he plays in the NFL. Recently, I ran into him, and I asked him, "Who's crying now?" We both laughed. That's the power of connection.

Lesson for Educators: Create Safe Spaces

Too often, when students struggle emotionally, teachers send them out of class. But sending them out is handing your power over to someone else. Why not develop your own connection and influence over the students you teach rather than allowing someone else to use their power and influence over *your* students? Keep your power by keeping them in the classroom and figuring out how to move them. The fact that others can influence the student to act differently shows that it can be done, so why would you not learn or develop that skill? Use that power. Come up with creative ways to manage students who need a little extra attention. For example, create a calm-down corner in your classroom—a place for students to go to when they need a quiet moment to self-regulate. Give them a signal they can use with you when they need a break, so they can just walk to the corner rather than having to explain themselves or feel exposed. Trust their self-awareness. Trust their process.

Before you ask, yes, the potential exists that some students might misuse that freedom. However, that's where professional judgment comes in. Education is a 'feeling' profession. You've got to *feel* for your students. Empathy isn't a weakness; it's a strength. It's what turns classrooms into communities. Every child has potential. Let's stop labeling them "hard to reach" and start reaching *harder*.

> **Science Snippet...**
> According to research on teacher-student relationships, students who perceive their teachers as empathetic are more likely to report a sense of belonging and emotional safety at school. That emotional connection can directly impact their academic success and overall well-being. Simply put, empathy opens the door to meaningful learning.[6]

Shifting the Label, Changing the Outcome

The bottom line here is that labels matter... especially the ones we place on children. When a student is called "hard to reach," that label doesn't stay in childhood. It follows them. I've seen it too many times: students who were once labeled "difficult" or "disengaged" as children grow into adults carrying that same identity. Often, those students are already facing deep challenges like poverty, trauma, or instability. Instead of finding support, the label becomes another barrier that holds them back, sometimes for life.

But let me remind you of the truth I've been asserting: no child is "hard to reach." Some children just need someone willing to go further to reach them.

As educators, we can shift this narrative by changing our language. Instead of labeling children, let's see them as an opportunity to serve. Each one is a chance to show up with compassion, to listen a little longer, and to lead with empathy. When we make that shift, we don't just change labels, we help to change lives.

WHAT'S THE MATTER?

When I pose the question, *"What's the matter?"* to educators, they often assume I'm talking about what is going wrong with an individual student, a child who wasn't meeting expectations, who was acting out or shutting down. *What's the matter with this kid?* But this question isn't just about one child's behavior. It is about everything surrounding that child, including the systems, the structures, and the policies that shape what happens in our schools. In light of this, the question becomes a broader, more pressing one: *What's the matter with the way we've allowed the heart of education to be buried beneath politics, policies, and bureaucracy?*

The signs are everywhere, from the school's front office to the headlines on the evening news. A lot of changes are taking place on the local, state, and national levels. Teachers and administrators, who give so much of themselves to their students, are stretched thin. Day after day, they are asked to do more with less—less time, less support, less compensation, and less understanding. They pour themselves into their classrooms, only to find that the system often gives little back. That constant strain doesn't just stay with the teachers, it trickles down. It becomes tension between teachers and students, frustration between teachers and administrators, and friction between school leaders and school boards. Somewhere along the way, we've drifted far from our original reason for being here: *the kids*.

So, what's the matter? The list is long and familiar to anyone in education. High-stakes testing has taken center stage, narrowing the focus of teaching to what can be measured. Rigid metrics have replaced meaningful learning. Teachers face overloaded schedules, understaffed classrooms, and salaries that fail to reflect their labor and expertise. Planning time has become a luxury rather than a standard. And collectively, all of this has contributed to a crisis: a nationwide teacher shortage. The very profession that makes all other professions possible is being abandoned in record numbers.

This really should be no surprise. There's no denying it: teachers are carrying more than ever before. The nationwide teacher shortage is real, and the weight educators are expected to bear is growing heavier by the day. They're not only responsible for teaching content; they're writing detailed lesson plans, managing students with significant trauma, leading after-school activities, and stepping into roles far beyond the classroom.

It's also the towering pile of responsibilities that extend far beyond the school day. It's the burnout that comes from working in a system that talks about data more than dreams. It's the absence of support and the constant feeling that no matter how much you give, it's never enough. These are the things that are "the matter." These are the barriers keeping us from doing the deeply human work of connecting with kids, and when we aren't connecting with kids, none of the other work we are doing really matters.

I've watched incredible educators—gifted, passionate, committed—pack up their classrooms on a Friday afternoon and walk away. Not because they didn't care, but because they were simply overwhelmed. Burnout is real. And if we want to keep great teachers in the profession, we have to take care of them. That starts with paying teachers what they're worth. But it also includes giving them time to breathe, mental health days built into the calendar, time to reflect and recharge. If we want teachers to do the heart work, we have to make sure their hearts are whole, too.

Further, when educators raise concerns, like when they say they need help, need rest, or need change, they're often met with familiar, dismissive responses: *"We can't offer incentives. There's no budget." "We don't have the staff." "We don't have the time."* These answers reinforce a dangerous mindset: that education is primarily about logistics, not people... that numbers matter more than names... that systems matter more than souls.

> ### Science Snippet...
> According to research from the RAND Corporation, a growing number of teachers are leaving the profession, with over 44% reporting they are likely to leave teaching within the next few years. The top reasons include stress, burnout, lack of support, and concerns about student behavior. Many also cite feeling undervalued and overwhelmed by non-instructional responsibilities that pull them away from the heart of teaching.[7]

If we want educators to pour into others, we have to make sure they're being poured into themselves. One of the most practical ways schools can support teachers is by embedding self-care into the culture—not as an afterthought, but as a priority. This could look like beginning faculty meetings with a mindfulness moment or scheduling professional development that includes yoga, meditation, or massage therapy sessions. Schools can even offer incentives for staff to participate in wellness activities or provide occasional release time specifically for self-care. When leaders make space for rest, it sends a powerful message: we value you, not just for what you do, but for who you are. Healthy teachers help build healthy school communities.

Ultimately, we've got to do better by our educators so that our educators can do better by our students. We can't afford to keep going down the same path. Our future is at stake! We have to come back to educators who are equipped to not only teach the lesson but reach the heart. We have to remind ourselves and our leaders, even those far removed in offices and big administrative buildings, that we are in *the kid business*. We are here to build futures. We are here to change lives.

Of course, we want students to be graduation-ready, college-bound, career-prepared, entrepreneurial, and employable. However, we won't achieve that objective unless we first stop and ask, *What's the matter?* Then, we must listen with openness and, with courage and clarity, *fix it*.

A Call to Action: Refocus, Reconnect, Restore

We can't care for students if we are too exhausted to care for ourselves. This chapter offers a call to action for all educators—not just teachers, but administrators, support staff, board members, and policymakers. We must stop treating self-care as an indulgence and start seeing it for what it is: a necessity. We cannot be strong for our students if we are running on empty. The first step toward restoring connection in schools is making space for educators to be whole, healthy, and heard.

But self-care alone isn't enough. We also need brave, honest conversations. We need teachers talking to teachers—not just about content, but about what's really going on. We need teachers and administrators communicating with respect and listening without defensiveness. We need school boards to not just hear the voices of educators but to *listen*—to truly take in the reality of what's happening on the ground.

Isolation is not a solution. Silence doesn't build trust. If we want to improve the student experience, we have to start by talking about what's getting in the way. We need shared problem-solving, not private suffering. I happen to believe the Bible, which teaches that confession and truth-telling lead to healing. In schools, healing happens when we are honest about our barriers and bold about change.

And while the issues we face are daunting, we are not powerless. There are steps we can take—real, actionable strategies that create movement and restore meaning to our work. We can reimagine school schedules to make space for true planning time—not just five minutes between meetings, but actual time to think, collaborate, and breathe. We can build in school-wide wellness practices: Friday reset moments, community circles, even simple acts of encouragement that remind us we are in this together.

We can form wellness and innovation committees—not as more tasks on someone's plate, but as opportunities for those who care deeply to lead change. There are always people willing to do the work. The key is to empower them, not burn them out.

We can make schools feel more like communities by involving our families. Hosting staff events that include spouses, partners, and children reminds everyone that we're not just employees; we're whole people. We can seek out grants and host fundraisers. We can invite parents to be partners, to contribute financially or through volunteering. Often, families want to help—they just need a clear path on how to do so, considering their limitations and pre-existing obligations.

> **Science Snippet...**
>
> A study published in the *Journal of Education Review Provision* found that parental involvement in a child's education is a significant predictor of academic success, regardless of the family's socioeconomic status. Engaged parents can positively influence their children's attitudes toward learning and school attendance.[8]

These steps won't solve everything. But they start something. They create forward motion. They remind us why we came to this profession in the first place—and why it's still worth fighting for.

Let the Main Thing Stay the Main Thing

No one enters this field for the perks. You didn't become a teacher, administrator, or board member because you were chasing a paycheck or counting down to summer break. You chose this work because you believed in something bigger. You wanted to make a difference. You wanted to light a spark. So, do it.

Be relentless in your advocacy for students. Don't let bureaucracy or burnout steal your fire. Be intentional about preserving your own light—because if you lose it, the whole room goes dark. Speak truth to power, even when it's uncomfortable. Keep coming back to the heart of the work, even when everything else tries to pull you away.

When stress starts to weigh you down, when the to-do list is too long, when the meetings are too many, and when the test scores are too low, pause and ask yourself, *What's the matter?* But don't stop there. Let that question lead you to action. Let it lead you to truth, because at the end of the day, what should matter most are the children. Always the children.

YES, THEY CAN!

Every child carries potential within them, but the way we talk about students doesn't always reflect that truth. Too often, we hear phrases like, "They can't read," when what's really meant is, "They can't read on grade level." There's an important distinction between those two statements. One leaves room for growth and possibility, while the other shuts the door. Words matter—deeply. When we shift how we speak about students, we begin to shift how we think about them. And even more importantly, we begin to shift what they believe about themselves.

> **Science Snippet...**
>
> A meta-analysis published in the *Journal of Educational Psychology* found that students who perceive their teachers as supportive are more likely to develop self-efficacy and motivation, leading to improved academic outcomes.[9]

This kind of casual judgment shows up in teacher lounges and faculty meetings more often than we'd like to admit. Comments like, "This is a good group," might seem harmless, but they carry weight. What are we really saying about the group that came before? That they weren't worth our time, our energy, or our best efforts? The truth is that students will rise—or fall—to meet the expectations we set. A "good group" isn't something that just shows up. It's the product of what we as educators pour into them. It's our preparation, our patience, and our belief that help a group thrive, not just the group itself.

From the Bottom to Belief

When I first became principal, our school was ranked near the bottom of the division. We were the lowest-performing campus, and morale was low. That first year, thirteen staff members left. Some of them simply didn't believe our students were capable. They said things like, "These kids can't do it," as if their challenges defined their ceiling. They pointed to poor test scores, chronic absenteeism, and chaotic home lives as reasons why our students were too far gone. A district leader even pulled me aside to ask, "Why are so many people leaving your school?" It was a fair question—but it had the wrong focus. Because the issue wasn't with the students. It was with belief.

By the next year, we were fully accredited. And no, the students didn't magically transform overnight. What changed was the mindset. I told my staff. "We have to make believers out of nonbelievers." I told the students the same thing: "They don't think you can pass—so what are we going to do about it?" We turned doubt into fuel. We made achievement personal. We held each other accountable. And slowly but surely, the belief began to spread. It was contagious. And it changed everything.

Belief Is a Practice

Believing in students isn't a slogan—it's a daily practice. It's not just saying, "Yes, they can"; it's showing up when it's hard, when the progress is slow, when the outcomes aren't guaranteed. Belief is what pushes a teacher to meet with a student every single day, even when that student is two or three grade levels behind. I've seen firsthand what faith and perseverance can do. The Bible teaches that with even a mustard seed amount of faith, mountains can move, and I've watched intentional, dedicated educators move more than a few. One real-life example that comes to mind is a fifth-grade student who was reading at a first-grade level. Her teacher didn't give up. She leaned in. She used every available resource, every spare moment, to pour into that child. By the end of the year, that student had gained two years of reading growth—and passed her standardized test. And she didn't just pass; she soared!

That's not magic. That's not luck. That's the power of belief combined with time, space, and encouragement to do what's needed. It's the result of a teacher who didn't see a label. She saw potential—and she refused to let go of it.

Giving Kids a Stage

Sometimes, all a student needs is a chance to shine—a moment where they feel seen for who they truly are. When I was the student government and Forensics/Debate sponsor, my classroom was often full of students, even those who weren't part of any club. They just wanted to be around the energy. One day, a student known more for his clowning than his classroom performance told me he could recite Dr. King's "I Have a Dream" speech. I didn't brush him off. I said, "Show me." And he did. He stood up and delivered it loud, proud, and powerful! The room went silent, then burst into applause. I told him, "You sound like a preacher." Thirty years later, he invited me to attend his ordination! That moment wasn't about a performance. It was about being seen. Being valued. Being given a platform. All because we gave him the stage.

Creating a Culture of Confidence

Creating belief in students doesn't happen by accident. It takes intentionality and consistency. As administrators, we have to go beyond the curriculum. Confidence isn't just built through lessons—it's built through culture. That's why we held pep rallies, organized class competitions, and made morning affirmations part of our daily rhythm. Our morning song was "Ain't No Stoppin' Us Now," because were on the move! These weren't gimmicks. They were strategies--tools of transformation.

I visited every classroom twice a day, even when I had district meetings or paperwork piled high. I made my walkthroughs non-negotiable. In the mornings, we'd chant lyrics together: *"Hopped up out the bed, turn my swag on, took a look in the mirror, said, 'What's up?"* That song by Soulja Boy became a rallying cry and point of connection between me and my students. It was simple, but it worked. It got them hyped. It helped them start their day feeling strong, confident, and ready. When students feel like they belong, they start to believe… and belief is where success begins.

Another way educators can use to powerfully shift their culture is through shifting the language used with the students. Moving from a mindset of saying "they can't" to saying "they can, with support" changes everything. When we speak belief into students, we begin to rewrite the narrative they tell themselves.

There's a small but mighty book called *Tongue Fu* that offers practical tips on how language can shape culture. One of the strategies it offers is as simple as replacing "but" with "and." It seems minor, but it makes a major difference. For example, instead of saying, "You did your homework, *but* you got two answers wrong," a teacher might say, "You did your homework, *and* you got 90% of the answers right!" That small adjustment affirms effort and builds confidence, rather than canceling it out. Words matter, so always use them to speak life.

I once had a meeting with a school leader who told me she had come in on a Saturday to prepare data showing why students at the school wouldn't pass the state assessments. I suggested that her time would have been better spent preparing strategies to help them succeed. For our students to believe in themselves, we must first demonstrate our confidence in them. Our words and actions should clearly communicate our fundamental belief: *Yes, they can!*

Leading by Showing Up

Leadership is not just about making decisions or reviewing data, it's about being present. I made it a point to be visible. During lunch, I'd head to the playground. Yes, even in heels. Even in the heat. Even when I was exhausted. I'd swing with the students—three pushes each. I'd go down the slides. And I made sure to rotate days, so every grade level got to see me.

When the first-grade teachers told me they were struggling with behavior, I didn't just give them tips from behind a desk. I showed up. I was there at recess. I watched. I supported. I let them know, "You're not alone." That's what leadership looks like. That's how we build a culture of belief—not just in students, but in each other.

> **Science Snippet...**
>
> A study published in the *American Journal of Education* found that when principals are consistently visible in hallways, classrooms, and common areas, students not only feel safer — they also behave better and perform better. Studies show that a principal's regular presence in the school environment builds trust, reinforces expectations, and fosters a stronger school climate. Students notice when leaders show up — and they respond with more positive behavior and academic outcomes.[10]

A Challenge to Educators: Let Them Surprise You

Saying "Yes, they can" isn't just a feel-good phrase. It's a daily commitment. It's the belief that no matter where a student starts, they can grow. They can rise. They can succeed—if we give them the tools and the space. And when we believe in them, they start to believe in themselves.

So, the next time a student seems off-track, resist the urge to write them off. Instead, say, "They're not there yet." Or, "They may need more support." Or even better, "They've got something in them we haven't seen—yet." Because when we say, "Yes, they can," we're not just talking about the future. We're helping shape it.

Also, by "we," allow me to remind you that it's not just us as educators; it's the entire ecosystem that needs to play a part in helping students believe in themselves and their capabilities to succeed academically. For example, one of the most effective ways to build a community around our students is by intentionally engaging families and local leaders in the life of the school. Family engagement nights offer powerful opportunities to do just that. Whether it's a cultural celebration, a Black History Month or other cultural showcase, or a math and science night where students get to shine and show what they've learned, these gatherings matter.

When I served as a principal, one of my favorite annual traditions was inviting families to join their children in painting ceiling tiles together around a shared theme. It wasn't just about art; it was about connection. Those ceiling tiles became symbols of belonging, ownership, and pride. When families are brought in and made to feel like partners, it reminds everyone that educating children is a shared responsibility and a shared joy.

THEY DON'T DRIVE!

5

There are many aspects of a student's life over which they have no control, yet too often, schools and educators punish them for circumstances beyond their reach. Consider how frequently students are labeled as "unmotivated," "irresponsible," or "not trying." The reality is far more complex. Many face barriers that would challenge even the most resilient adults. Chronic absenteeism is one clear example. While schools and teachers now track attendance as a key benchmark, how can we hold a child accountable for missing school if there is no bus available or if their parent's work schedule makes timely transportation impossible? Simply put, students don't drive. They don't have control over the logistics of getting themselves to school or over many of the decisions that impact their attendance. Yet, we often treat them as if they do.

Stop Blaming. Start Understanding.

Imagine a little boy walking into class late—again. The typical response might be a reprimand: "You're late… *again*. You already missed half of the reading block." But what that child hears is not just criticism; they hear shame, which only adds to their burden. Instead of assuming failure before the day even begins, educators should focus on welcoming students and helping them catch up once they arrive. They should avoid criticizing parents because when parents are criticized, the children internalize that judgment. The truth is that a child might be late because their mom works multiple jobs and simply overslept. They might live in a home where transportation is unreliable or unsafe, or where simply getting out the door each morning is a struggle. When students enter a school building, from the front office to their classroom, they deserve to feel welcomed, not worn down by blame.

Empathy Over Assumptions

Educators often unintentionally compound the struggles students face by adding judgment to the mix. When a student is already contending with challenges beyond their control, the last thing they need is to be judged, gossiped about, or dismissed. We don't always know the full story. A student might lack school supplies—not out of laziness, but because their family can't afford extras. They may appear tired not from late-night video games but because their home environment is chaotic or overcrowded. We must remember that students do not control the narrative of their lives, but what we say and do can empower them to begin taking control. Our words and actions can be the first steps toward helping them "take the wheel."

> ### Science Snippet...
> Studies show that teachers trained in empathetic communication see a significant decrease in classroom disruptions and an increase in student cooperation. Empathy doesn't mean lowering expectations; it means seeing the student, not just the behavior.[11]

Flip the Script

Instead of punishing students for absences, schools should creatively and compassionately reward presence. Some schools have introduced "Present Patrols," a kind of attendance celebration similar to a sweepstakes, where principals and staff visit homes with pizza or small gifts to recognize students who have improved their attendance, even if they previously struggled. Other schools hold attendance shout-outs, create photo walls featuring students with their "special someone," or offer clubs and activities that students don't want to miss. It also helps to employ methods like requesting late bus transportation and walking through the neighborhoods of students who are chronically absent (those who miss class at least once a week). While incentives can motivate, it's even more important to build a culture that says, *We want you here. We need you here. You matter here.*

Real Stories, Real Shifts

One story that stays with me is about a particular mother who didn't drive and struggled to get her child to school consistently. When we needed her to come for a meeting, we picked her up, bringing her three children along—complete with a car seat for the youngest. That simple act of kindness changed everything. From that day forward, her child attended school regularly unless they were sick. Later, when we opened a new school in her zone, she came proudly and told me she would be there every day. Despite living in public housing with concrete floors, her home was immaculate, and she was proud. That experience reminded me how wrong assumptions can be. If I had let judgment guide me instead of empathy, I would have missed one of the most meaningful home visits I ever made.

Watch Your Words

The language we use about and to students matters deeply. Changing the ways in which we speak can create a more supportive environment. Instead of asking, "Why were you out?" say, "I missed you." Replace "You're always late" with "I'm glad you're here."

This shift in language should be a core part of staff development, emphasizing professional and positive communication, as well as restorative conversations. When students know they will be welcomed warmly, they are more likely to show up.

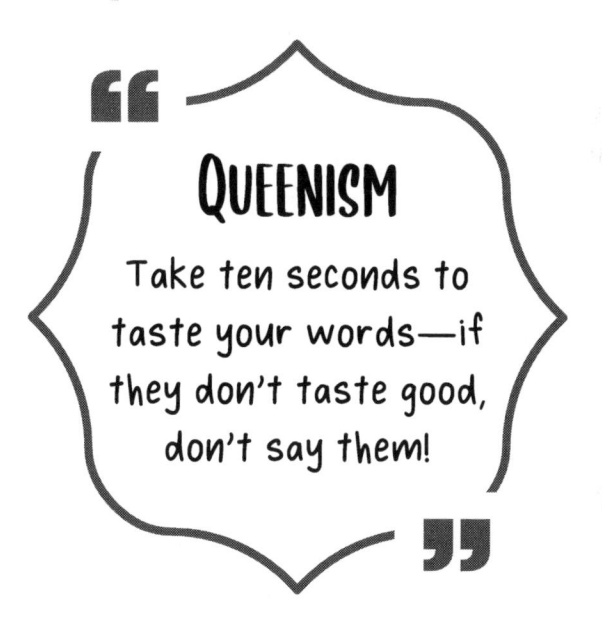

> **QUEENISM**
> Take ten seconds to taste your words—if they don't taste good, don't say them!

Build the Drive

At one faculty meeting, teachers complained about tardiness. I responded, "No, we have to do something." Together, we worked with parents, encouraged scheduling appointments after school and adjusted our tone and approach. The truth is, while students may not be driving their lives yet, if we do our job well, they will eventually take the wheel—steering their own futures. Therefore, we must stop judging the child who leaves early because their parent must get to work, stop scolding the student who's late because they don't have a car, and stop dismissing the hungry, tired, or unprepared—because those circumstances are not their choice.

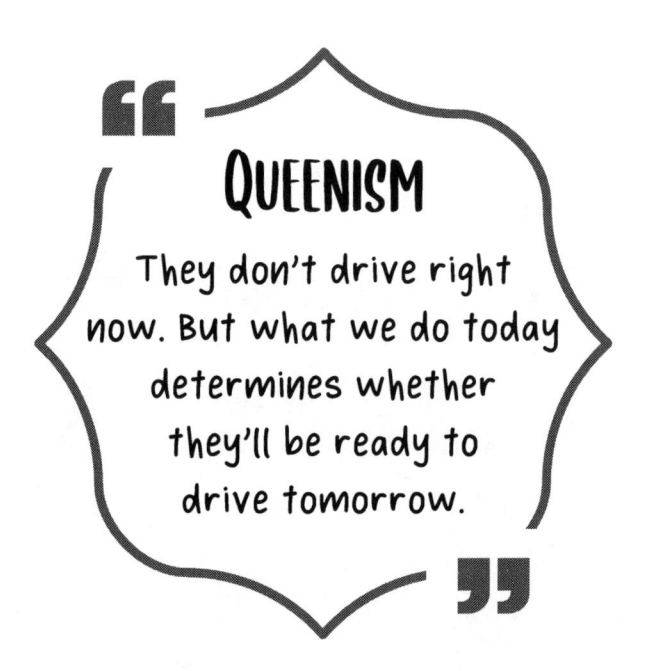

> **QUEENISM**
>
> They don't drive right now. But what we do today determines whether they'll be ready to drive tomorrow.

THE PARENT APPEAL

One of the most persistent concerns in K–12 education is low parental involvement. Educators often lament that parents don't attend conferences, skip PTA meetings, or fail to participate in school events. But before labeling families as disengaged, we must reflect on how we're defining "involvement." Too often, schools present a narrow, one-size-fits-all model of participation, failing to recognize the realities and limitations that many families face. A parent working night shifts may not be able to attend a PTA meeting, but they might be more than willing to cut out decorations for a school program or send in snacks for a class trip. The question isn't whether families want to be involved—it's whether we're giving them a way to contribute that actually fits into their lives.

We also tend to see only the parents of high-achieving students—the ones whose children earn consistently good grades—while struggling families may not appear at traditional school events. But that doesn't mean they don't care. We have to meet them where they are. I've met parents at ball games, in grocery stores, and even in car lines during drop-off. I've said, "Hey, I wanted to talk to you—did you know your child is having a little trouble in math?" That one small moment builds a bridge. I've exchanged numbers right there and followed up with text updates. It's not about pushing paperwork—it's about personal connections. Parents respond when they feel seen, not judged.

Real engagement begins with a simple question: *Do I want to connect with this family?* The "want-to" spirit is where transformation starts. Parents know when outreach is genuine. They can tell when a teacher cares deeply—when they give out their number and say, "Call me if your child doesn't understand something at home." That kind of trust can last for years. I once hired a teacher whose former students still reach out to her decades later, one of whom is now a professional athlete. That kind of relationship is built on trust, consistency, and sincerity.

> **Science Snippet...**
>
> Research from the Education Endowment Foundation suggests that parental engagement can lead to an average of four months' additional progress in students' academic achievement. Tailoring communication to encourage positive dialogue about learning can enhance this effect.[12]

Every child wants their parent or someone they love to show up for them. I've stood in auditoriums and gymnasiums and seen the quiet pain on children's faces when no one came to see them get an award or perform at an event. It breaks your heart. That's why I always made sure to have extra volunteers—stand-in "dads" for the Daddy-Daughter Dance, mentors, and community members. When a child has someone in their corner, even if it's not a biological parent, they stand taller. Research confirms what we know instinctively: family engagement—however it looks—boosts academic success and emotional well-being. And it doesn't always require much. Sometimes it's as simple as showing up, sending a note, or asking, "How can I help?"

Incentives can also be powerful tools—but only when they feel authentic, not transactional. A certificate of recognition for a parent who donates supplies or a joint award for students and parents who collaborate on a project can send the message that all contributions matter. Sometimes, it's the very act of *asking* a parent to be involved that changes everything. It tells them, "You're wanted here." I avoid guilt tactics, like saying, "Your child really wants you to be there," because while that might motivate, it can also deepen shame. We don't know what experiences parents bring from their own school years. We want them to come because they *want* to be part of their child's journey, not because they feel coerced.

One of my favorite ways to connect was through Sunday messages. Every weekend, I'd send out a quick facetime video to families about what was coming up that week. One time I skipped sending the video because it was Thanksgiving; I didn't want to disrupt the families' holiday celebrations. That Monday, a little boy came up to me and said, "You didn't call us last night!" He truly believed that my message was just for *him*. And because he believed it, I knew his mother was listening, too. Even brief messages can nurture trust and help parents feel in the loop.

When I noticed a concerning number of students earning Ds and Fs midyear, I didn't wait for the end of the semester. I invited parents to come in—not to shame them, but to offer help. We handed out work packets, offered tutoring plans, and brought in counselors. We created a space that said, *You're not in this alone.* This wasn't some pre-scheduled event—it was responsive, and it worked. Parents left those meetings feeling empowered, not embarrassed.

I once inherited an elementary school ranked among the lowest in academic performance. I was told not to expect much—certainly not full accreditation in a year. But I refused to accept that. I banned unnecessary student removals from class and got in those classrooms myself, offering feedback and support. Thirteen teachers asked for transfers. A higher-up asked why so many wanted out, and I said, "Maybe if they leave, the school will succeed." And we did. With the right staff, heart, and belief in students, despite the socioeconomic status of our school or our history, we got accredited. That achievement lifted not just the school, but the whole community.

Building parent partnerships isn't limited to the school building. I've gone to church services when students were getting baptized. I've done home visits. I've even ridden the school bus, one time to address student behavior issues and another just to meet a parent waiting at the bus stop. I hopped on the bus at the school, saw the parent there to meet their child at the bus stop, got off the bus to chat with them for a few minutes, got back on the bus, and rode it back to the school. These small efforts speak volumes. They say, "We see you. We're in this together." And the truth is, many parents appreciate the effort more than we realize. It's not the grand gestures that win them over; it's the consistent, quiet presence. I believe God works through the quiet, steady things like faithfulness, consistency, and small seeds of effort that grow in time. That's how trust is built, too.

Michelle McQueen Williams, Ph.D.

> ### Science Snippet...
> Decades of research compiled by the American Psychological Association show that parental involvement in education improves student attendance, social skills, and behavior. Engaged parents can help children adapt better to school and foster a positive learning environment.[13]

Building trust, especially with families who have experienced educational trauma, takes time and care. We can't just talk about open-door policies; we have to mean it. I've told parents who showed up in the school office to talk to me just before it was time for me to go make my morning rounds, "Don't leave! I want to hear what you have to say. I'll be with you as soon as I make my rounds." I made it a point to remember their names and their lives. "Ms. Johnson, are you still working the third shift?" Small acknowledgments like that make people feel seen, respected, and welcomed. They make them feel significant. They show that you actually care.

Further, the care must be ongoing. Once, a woman shared with me that her mother had passed away and her daughter had just had a baby. I'd figured that something was going on when someone else started picking up her child. Why? Because years earlier, that same parent told me her mother had been ill. When we truly *know* our students and families, we notice changes. We notice distraction and worry. We notice sadness. We notice pain. And we can respond with empathy, not judgment. As a Christian, I've learned that "mourning with those who mourn," or empathizing with them through their difficulties, isn't optional; it's essential. Leading with the heart in mind responds with compassion in moments like these.

Parental engagement is not just about attending events. It's about trust, visibility, consistency, and love. It starts with believing that every family has something valuable to offer— and creating space for them to offer it in their own way.

IT'S ABOUT THEM

After more than 35 years of working with students and families, I have learned one vital truth: we must always keep the main thing the main thing. Everything we do in education should center on the children—their dreams, their futures. If they have a strong foundation and a bright future, then our society will have a better future as well. This work is not about us. We adults have had opportunities, but the students are the ones who need them now. I often tell teachers, "We have jobs. They have to get them." I love teachers, but I love students even more because it is ultimately about them—their hopes, their goals, and how we can support their journey. This is hard work, and if we truly believe education is about the kids, then it is the work we *must* do.

Beyond Scores: Remembering the Child

Sometimes it's easy to lose sight of this. When we look at test scores, attendance rates, or graduation percentages, we might forget that behind every number is a child's life. If a school's test score is 40%, that means 40% of the students are struggling—children. And if it's 100%, that means every child is succeeding. The focus should never be on the numbers themselves, but on the individual growth of each student. They won't all reach the mark at the same time, but they should all be moving forward, growing.

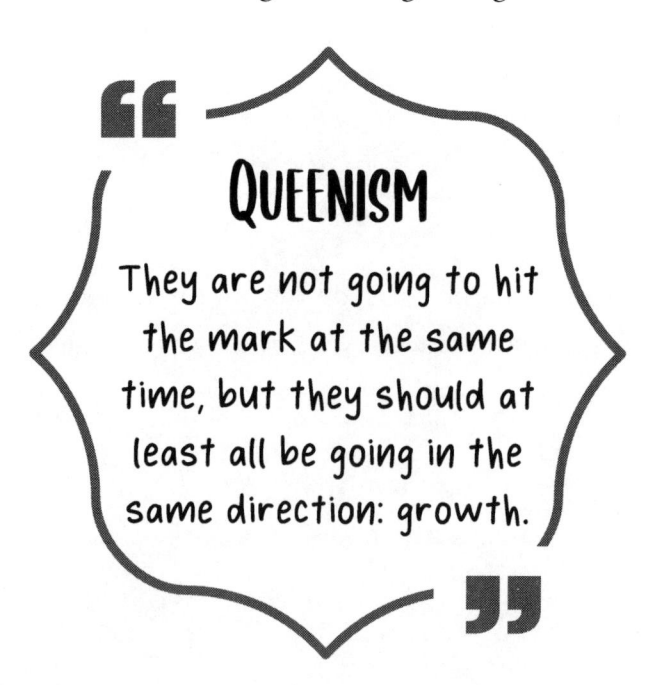

> **QUEENISM**
>
> They are not going to hit the mark at the same time, but they should at least all be going in the same direction: growth.

Love and Expectation: The Heart of Student-Centered Leadership

I would be remiss not to refer to a concept I introduced in my first book, *Leadership in Three Words*, as I share my insights in this chapter, *It's About Them*. That concept is the principle of Love and Expectation, and it deserves a place in any conversation centered around putting students first.

At its core, Love and Expectation is the idea that we must care deeply for our students while also challenging them to rise to their full potential. It's easy to show love to students who are well-behaved, eager to learn, and follow directions—but real leadership is revealed when we extend that same love to students who are struggling, resistant, or harder to reach. That's when love becomes a choice, not just a feeling. And that's also where expectation must walk hand in hand with care. To love students is to hold them to a high standard, not despite their challenges, but because of them.

You cannot say you love children and then allow them to drift through the day disengaged, unnoticed, or underestimated. I've seen it too many times—students with their heads down, disconnected from the lesson, and teachers continuing on as if those students aren't even there. That is not love. That is not expectation. When we love students, we notice them. We ask why they're checked out. We meet a need if we can. And then we make it clear that we expect them to be present, to participate, and to grow.

This principle has been a non-negotiable in every building I've led and every class I've taught whether k-12 or higher ed. Every adult, whether a classroom teacher, a support staff member, or a school leader, has a responsibility to love our students enough to expect something of them. Even when life is hard. Even when we're carrying our own burdens. We don't have the luxury of checking out on our students just because we're having a bad day. The children need us to show up, fully present, with hearts open and expectations held high.

When we talk about *It's About Them*, this is what we mean. They deserve our best. All of them. Not just the compliant ones. Not just the ones who are easy to love. Every child should feel seen, valued, and challenged. That's what Love and Expectation looks like in action—and that's what it means to lead and teach with students truly at the center.

The Power of Relationships

Each child walks into the classroom carrying different traumas, experiences, and challenges. What we do, and sometimes what we fail to do, impacts them deeply. Teaching isn't just about delivering content; it's about making a difference in their lives. When I ask students to name their favorite and least favorite teachers, what stands out isn't what they taught; it's how they made them feel. The teachers who believed in them and made space for them to grow remain memorable. The teachers who led with care and understanding, allowing them to come early or stay late to finish their homework before practice are the ones whose names come to their minds. Those small acts of care mattered. That's why I open every class with a quote about relationships—because relationships matter. Students will engage with the content when they know you genuinely care about them.

Embracing the Hard Days

Teaching is tough. There will be hard days, days when nothing seems to go right. I encourage educators to journal and reflect—not just on the challenges but on the good moments, too. Those good days, when a student returns and says, "I remember you and how you made me feel," will outweigh the hard days. It is in those moments that you know you have truly made a difference. So, take the good with the bad, and keep coming back.

Walking With Students Through Graduation

I recall a time as an assistant principal when we started working with a cohort of ninth graders and stayed with them through their senior year. Ninth grade was a challenging year; failure rates were high. To support the students, we created attendance parties and quarterly grade consultations and hosted clubs and step teams to engage them. We let the students take ownership of their graduation, planning who would speak and organizing the choir. They did it themselves. I was just the guide. On graduation day, the students walked down a large hill, wearing their caps and gowns, toward their seats. Seeing those young people—many of whom had been counted out by society—cross that hill was an emotional, beautiful sight. It was the largest graduation the school had seen in years. Although the morning was rainy and cloudy, the sun broke through just in time for the ceremony. It felt like the world was shining on them, affirming their achievement. Every parent wants to see their child graduate, and that day, the whole community celebrated.

It's About Them, Not Us

We are here to serve the children, to help them get the futures they deserve. This requires thinking out of the box and going the extra mile. Be warned: when you introduce new ideas, there will always be pushbacks. Some say if you spend too much time with students, you're micromanaging. If you stay in the office, you're hiding. But I will say to my dying day, adults have jobs—they have responsibilities—but we also have a sacred duty to ensure students have the future they want. Whether that future includes entrepreneurship, college, or any other path, we must support them every step of the way. And I want to see every single one of them get across that hill and walk across that stage, proud and accomplished. I believe it honors God when we help students walk into the fullness of who they were created to be: whole, hopeful, and ready.

> **QUEENISM**
>
> The school building is not built for us educators to have jobs; it is built for the students to get jobs!

THE LEADERSHIP CHALLENGE:

Get Your Mind Focused on the Heart of the Work

In this journey through leadership three *more* words at a time, we've returned again and again to the heart. Not just sentimentally, but intentionally. Because this work, this calling of education, is and always has been about people, and people are not robots. They have souls, hearts, and emotions, and they need things like connection and care if you are going to be effective in anything you do with them.

This work is about the children who walk into our classrooms each day with dreams and needs. It's about the families who love them. And it's about the educators who show up, day after day, to guide, nurture, and lead with heart in mind.

We began this book by going heart to heart. We named what matters most: connection. Not programs. Not paperwork. But people. Relationships are not extras in this work; they *are* the work. And from that foundation, we acknowledged what so many educators experience: the struggle of reaching students who've been labeled "hard to reach." But what we discovered is that those very students are often just guarding wounded hearts, waiting for someone to see them, to believe in them, to try again.

Then we asked the hard question, *What's the matter?* and we didn't shy away from the uncomfortable answers. Overloaded systems. Disconnected structures. Educators burning out under the weight of metrics that forget the human side of learning. But we didn't stop there. We called for restoration: a return to the heart, to community, to purpose. Because when we remember why we came to this work, we remember who it's for, and it's not for us and our own comfort and convenience.

We re-centered the conversation with a bold declaration: Yes, they can. Every child, regardless of background, income, or label, can achieve. But not without leaders who see their brilliance before it's fully formed. Not without teachers who refuse to give up. And yes, we must be willing to challenge our systems, to shift our mindsets, and to reimagine what support really looks like. Because if we believe they can, then we must act like it.

And then we got practical. They don't drive. That simple truth reminded us that students don't control most of what happens to them. They rely on us—adults—to create safe, welcoming, inclusive environments. Environments that offer more than discipline and data points. Spaces that reflect joy, consistency, accountability, and love.

But we also remembered something else: students don't walk this path alone. Families matter. Chapter 6 brought us face-to-face with the reality that parental engagement isn't about event attendance or PTA meetings. It's about connection, respect, and opportunity. It's about meeting parents where they are and believing—*truly* believing—that every family has something to offer. When we do that work with sincerity, when we extend our hand without judgment, families show up in their own way, in their own time, and with deep impact.

Finally, we arrived at the heart of it all: It's about them. The children. Every decision, every strategy, every shift we make must keep the main thing the main thing. It's not about our convenience, our traditions, or our comfort zones. It's about their future. As I said, they're not going to hit the mark at the same time—but they should all be growing. That's our charge.

So where do we go from here?

We stay in the work. We keep leading, not with titles or authority, but with compassion and courage. We listen harder. We love deeper. We show up, *especially* on the hard days. And when the path forward feels uncertain or overwhelming, we pause, we breathe, and we ask ourselves the question that has guided us from the beginning: What's the matter? Then, with resolve, we do something about it. So, what, now what?

At the end of the day, when the classrooms are quiet and the buses have pulled away, what matters most are the children. Their growth. Their hope. Their future. Let that always be the reason we teach and lead. With heart. With courage. With purpose. Let that always be the main thing.

"Queenisms"
Leadership in Three MORE Words

- "They made it to college—now they need help making it through college."
- "Little people grow up to be big people that somehow made it to college."
- "Teaching is a feeling business. It is how we make students feel that makes them think."
- "Some students need grace before they ever give us growth."
- "Take ten seconds to taste your words—if they don't taste good, don't say them!"
- "They don't drive right now. But what we do today determines whether they'll be ready to drive tomorrow."
- "They are not going to hit the mark at the same time, but they should at least all be going in the same direction: growth."
- "The school building is not built for us educators to have jobs; it is built for the students to get jobs!"

"Queenisms"
Leadership in Three Words

- "When you change the language, you change the culture!"

- "You're not going to make a paycheck off the backs of these kids!"

- "Let data drive your decisions. Behind every set of numbers is a story waiting to be told. Every score represents a person and his/her needs."

- "Stand and deliver! Sometimes, you have to stand up and say the tough things that people don't want to hear."

- "Whether it's a good or bad decision or a successful or unsuccessful program, everything points back to the leader who writes, nurtures, and rolls out the vision!"

- "You won't need to do damage control if you do your due diligence!"

- "Leadership is the invisible rope that pulls other people to greatness. They don't even know they are being pulled!"

- "I love teaching, but I love kids more!"

- "We don't teach content; we teach children!"
- "Don't hire fast. Hire well!"
- "There is an art and a science to leadership."
- "If you see something, say something!"

ABOUT THE AUTHOR

During her career as a professional educator, Reverend Dr. Michelle Kelly McQueen-Williams has shown a deep concern for the educational, social, and emotional well-being of the children she has encountered as a teacher, assistant principal, and elementary principal for Henrico County Public schools. She was named the first principal of Harvie Elementary, the 45th elementary school to be opened in Eastern Henrico County. Dr. McQueen-Williams recently retired as the Director of Elementary Education in Henrico County Public Schools. Since retiring, she has served as Interim Dean in the Evelyn Reid Syphax School of Education at her alma mater, Virginia Union University. She currently serves as Executive Director of P-12 experiences and educational initiatives at Virginia Union University. In addition, she is an executive leadership coach. Dr. McQueen serves as a Leadership Supervisor for the University of Richmond's Educational Leadership and Policy Studies Division.

McQueen-Williams is a product of the Richmond Public School System and holds a Bachelor of Arts degree in Journalism from Virginia Union University (where she was crowned Miss Virginia Union University), a Master's degree and a Ph.D. in Educational Leadership from Virginia Commonwealth University, and a certificate of completion from Virginia Tech's Aspiring Superintendent's program. Dr. McQueen-Williams graduated with honors from the Samuel Dewitt Proctor School of Theology at Virginia Union University with her Master of Divinity. Dr. McQueen serves the board of directors as Vice President of the Henrico Police Athletic League. Dr. McQueen was recently honored with the Cornerstone Award of the John W. Barco Chapter Alumnae Chapter of Virginia Union University. She is also the recipient of the Mary McCleod Bethune Award from the National Council of Negro Women-Chesterfield Chapter. She is a Diamond Life Member of Delta Sigma Theta and serves as chaplain of the Chesterfield Alumnae Chapter. Licensed and ordained, McQueen-Williams currently is an Associate Minister at the First Baptist Church of South Richmond, where the Reverend Drs. Dwight C. and Derik E. Jones are the pastors. Civic minded, she seeks to motivate, empower, and inspire all with whom she comes in contact.

ENDNOTES

1 National Center for Education Statistics (NCES). (2022). "The Nation's Report Card: 2022 Reading and Mathematics Assessments." https://nces.ed.gov/nationsreportcard/

2 Schonert-Reichl, K. A. (2017). Social and emotional learning and teachers. *The Future of Children*, 27(1), 137–155. https://doi.org/10.1353/foc.2017.0007

3 Gillet, N., Vallerand, R. J., & Lafrenière, M.-A. K. (2012). Intrinsic and extrinsic school motivation as a function of age: A self-determination theory perspective. *Journal of Educational Psychology*, 104(4), 1043–1054. Carmody, D. P., & Lewis, M. (2006). Brain activation when hearing one's own and others' names. *Brain Research*, 1116(1), 153–158.

4 American Psychological Association. (n.d.). *Teacher-student relationships.* https://www.apa.org/education-career/k12/relationships

5 American Psychological Association. (n.d.). *Teacher-student relationships.* https://www.apa.org/education-career/k12/relationships

6 Cornelius-White, J. (2007). Learner-centered teacher-student relationships are effective: A meta-analysis. *Review of Educational Research*, 77(1), 113–143. https://doi.org/10.3102/003465430298563

7 RAND Corporation. (2022). "Teachers Are Not Okay: How the COVID-19 Pandemic Is Damaging Teachers' Mental Health." https://www.rand.org/pubs/research_reports/RRA1108-1.html

8 Utazi, B. U. (2023). *The role of parental involvement in children's education and academic performance: A review of literature.* PhilArchive. https://philarchive.org/archive/UTATRO

9   Roorda, D. L., Koomen, H. M. Y., Spilt, J. L., & Oort, F. J. (2011). *The influence of affective teacher–student relationships on students' school engagement and achievement: A meta-analytic approach.* Review of Educational Research, 81(4), 493–529. https://www.sciencedirect.com/science/article/pii/S0001691825001015

10 Horng, E. L., Klasik, D., & Loeb, S. (2010). Principal time-use and school effectiveness. *American Journal of Education,* 116(4), 491–523.
https://doi.org/10.1086/653625

11 Weinstein, R. S., & Novodvorsky, I. (2010). *Middle and Secondary Classroom Management: Lessons from Research and Practice.* McGraw-Hill.

12 Education Endowment Foundation. (n.d.). *Parental engagement.* https://educationendowmentfoundation.org.uk/education-evidence/teaching-learning-toolkit/parental-engagement

13 Annie E. Casey Foundation. (2014, July 24). *Parental involvement is key to student success, research shows.* https://www.aecf.org/blog/parental-involvement-is-key-to-student-success-research-shows

Made in the USA
Middletown, DE
07 July 2025